THE OLIVE OIL
HANDBOOK

Cooking and
Baking with the
Liquid Gold of
the
Mediterranean

Marisa
Rinaldi

TABLE OF CONTENTS

INTRODUCTION

Why Olive Oil is "Liquid Gold"

Go to any kitchen in the Mediterranean region, from the sun-soaked shores of Sicily to the azure coastlines of Greece and you are sure to find, prominently displayed like liquid treasure, a bottle of olive oil.

Far more than just a cooking fat, olive oil infuses Mediterranean life, culture, cuisine, and identity. It has captivated mankind for millennia with its versatility, flavors, and unparalleled health properties bestowed by the olive tree.

Olive oil's history in the region traces back thousands of years. The origins of olive tree cultivation are lost to antiquity, with evidence pointing back to nearly 6000 years when early peoples likely began growing olive trees using selections from wild-growing stock.

We know the Ancient Egyptians used olive oil in food, lighting fuels, medicines, and mummification rituals by 3000 BC.

As civilizations flourished around the Mediterranean basin over the centuries that followed, from Greece and Rome, around North Africa and the Levant, to Spain and other European cultures, the olive tree ascended in meaning and importance, finding its way into religious texts, mythology and lore.

Its oil became an invaluable cooking staple, fuel for lamps, and "liquid gold" that could build wealth and power.

By the time of the Roman Empire, olive cultivation had spread prolifically, with sophisticated production techniques and trade in the prized oil reaching its zenith. Author and olive oil expert Carol Firenze noted in her book "Olive Oil: A Gourmet Guide" that the Romans so revered good olive oil that they would bury jars of oil with their dead to take into the afterlife.

When the Roman Empire eventually faded, olive oil production fell into decline for some centuries in Western Europe. Yet the enduring cultural legacy around the Mediterranean, especially in the east, never erased the olive tree from regional significance nor fully diminished its cultivation over time.

Today, the countries ringing the Mediterranean Sea account for 98% of worldwide olive production. Over 750 million olive trees continue to be meticulously tended, some ancient specimens standing as links to history with trunks so wide five grown men hand-to-hand cannot encircle them.

Other younger orchards are leading a resurgence, using the latest methods to improve fruit yields and oil quality. Some small groves cling to hillsides in time-honored traditional fashion while massive super-high density farms churn out olive oil on a vast scale. Ancient stone mills still used for small-batch oils co-exist with modern stainless steel pressing equipment able to process tons of olives at one time.

This abundance enables the Mediterranean zone to produce nearly 2.7 million tons of olive oil annually (as of 2020), with Europe, North Africa, Turkey, Syria, Lebanon Palestine, and Jordan representing the majority share.

For all the evolution in olive farming and processing over the millennia, what has not changed is the region's attachment to olive oil for its beloved flavors, its role in cultural identity, and its importance not just in the kitchen but in family rituals, agricultural livelihoods and economic impacts.

This book celebrates ALL the faces of olive oil in the lands where its heritage lies, as a cooking staple of course, but also as medicine, cosmetics, fuel for lamps, spiritual anointing oil, and the crop validating small farmers' dedication year after year despite struggles or scarcity.

We will dive into olive oil's history, geography, varieties, uses and future trajectory. You cannot fully grasp Mediterranean cuisine, agriculture, or customs without understanding olive oil's contributions which have quietly shaped societies around this sea since before history was recorded on parchment.

A Precious Natural Resource

What makes olive oil so special that it has persisted as a regional treasure for millennia? How has it continually captured attentions, taste buds, and imaginations of generation after generation?

For one, it is incredibly versatile in uses. The same oil that may be drizzled into a Greek salad or over pasta aglio e olio as a finish, can also be blessed by clergy, mixed into natural skin creams and soaps, or used to polish leather and wood or lubricate machinery.

It can fuel oil lamps or Menorah candles during religious ceremonies as it has done for ages instead of exotic spices found along Mediterranean trade routes.

Its flavor profile is also complex, ranging from peppery and pungent to mildly fruity and buttery depending on the olive variety, time of harvest, processing methods and age or storage. It lends a unique character to dishes that seed- and nut-based oils cannot replicate.

But olive oil's popularity stems first and foremost from the copious health and wellness benefits biology built right into this oil, naturally protecting it from spoilage. Its robust antioxidants and anti-inflammatory oleocanthal phytochemicals are associated with reduced risk for nearly every common health ailment at some level.

From fighting cardiovascular disease, regulating cholesterol, and supporting organ function, to protecting the skin from UV radiation damage and protecting brain health, olive oil is one of the most stable, nutritious, medicinally-potent plant oils one could ingest.

Olive oil's concentration of biologically active compounds, some only recently discovered by science, is unmatched by other oils. Researchers continue to reveal new ways olive oil nourishes human wellness.

The environmental resilience of the olive tree in often arid, marginal growing regions around the Mediterranean basin is equally laudable. Olive trees thrive on hillsides and heat where other fruit trees cannot bear up. Evergreens, survive and produce even through drought cycles with little irrigation owing to their robust root structures. The trees are hardy, long-lived and can grow up to 100 feet tall and 50 feet wide, producing reliable yields for decades, even centuries.

Olive trees begin fruiting at about 5-6 years from planting but optimal oil yields generally start around 12-15 years in. Remarkably some olive trees in the Mediterranean region have been alive since ancient Roman times thanks to tender cultivation practices passed down through generations that value sustainability.

Beyond impeccable survivor biology, the olive harvest cycle itself and customary extraction methods yield a high-quality, aromatic oil boasting an array of phytonutrients. Unlike mass commodity vegetable oils, olive oil is made by simply crushing or pressing whole fruit, without the use of heat or solvent chemicals that damage nutrients. Fruit ripeness and ideal timing of harvest are paramount.

Cultivating healthy olive trees and meticulous fruit handling standards also ensure an oil full of flavor and health qualities nature intended. This is why standards and certifications related to production estimates become so imperative for guaranteeing quality across the olive oil industry, as we will discuss later.

Without diligent growing and picking of drupes at their peak with careful, rapid processing, olive oil can quickly turn from gold to fodder.

Pride of the Mediterranean

For olive growers, both small and large scale farmers, olive oil is far more than a commodity or export product. It is the lifeblood of tradition and family heritage. Olive oil production remains one of the most important agricultural activities in the Mediterranean - economically, socially, and environmentally.

According to reporting by the International Olive Council, the countries belonging to the Mediterranean basin produce 95% of the world's olive oil and account for 85% of the world's table olives. Over 2,538,000 family farms in the region cultivate olive trees across roughly 5 million hectares of land. And market value continues to grow. As of 2020, the global olive oil trade was valued at $22 billion with estimates pointing to over $32 billion by 2027.

The leading producers in metric tons are Spain, Italy, Greece and Portugal respectively. However, consumption remains highest in Italy followed by Greece and Spain. This reveals how olive oil definitively permeates regional food cultures.

Beyond impressive production and export figures, however, lies cultural meaning that statistics cannot capture. Olive oil is the lifeblood of heritage. It brings families together during the November olive harvest, a festive time preceding the holidays.

Children playing and grandparents singing during harvest amid the olive nets create lasting memories and set foundations. The first pressing of each harvest's yield, often using family or village-owned small groves, is set aside for the home table rather than a quick bulk sale. Special meals are prepared for the workers who help hand harvest.

Most olive oil producing regions have their own festivals and customs honoring olive oil's importance to work, food, and unity. Olive oil is shared between friends and gifted for celebrations. It is as symbolic of regional artisanship and identity as wine in France or cheese in in the Netherlands. And just as award-winning vineyards hold esteem for their vintages, olive oil producers take immense pride in the oils their family trees produce.

Increasingly they utilize industrial appellation systems to verify geographic origin and specialty production practices. Some feel another olive oil renaissance has been underway across parts of Europe and the pan-Mediterranean region over the past two decades. While globalization and corporatization of agriculture threatening food traditions - from Castile to Crete - small producers, boutique growers, olive oil tourism outfits, specialty harvest equipment makers, and oil-centric epicureans continually raise the stakes on quality.

This is seen through the sheer variety of olive oils available today emphasizing freshness, single estate terroir, and discerning production practices that honor the spectrum of heritage olives unique to microclimates and villages. There are thousands of boutique labels to explore based on priorities ranging from smooth and buttery to robust and peppery.

Enthusiasts embrace discussion about ideal serving temperatures to best experience flavor subtleties, pairing oils with dishes to accentuate regional ingredient combinations, or debating the need for designations like Protected Designation of Origin (PDO) to verify quality standards. Annual olive oil competitions judged by expert panels now operate like wine tasting events to award top tier Extra Virgin Olive Oils (EVOO).

Specialty olive oil bars found abroad in Atlanta, NYC, Toronto, Paris and elsewhere let patrons sample various single cultivar oils' aromatic qualities from different growing areas before selecting their favorite bottle to take home.

Chefs proudly display bottles of artisanal olive oil on restaurant tables for dipping bread just as fine estate wines are decanted tableside. Travel literature and culinary shows expound on olive oil oriented excursions that let foodies and eco-tourists see groves firsthand, experience harvest traditions, learn regional styles of production - from tree pruning methods to milling equipment - and fully appreciate olive oil's continuing influence across economies, foodways and cultural traditions that run soul-deep in nations touched by the Mediterranean.

The allure of pure, ethically-sourced, small farm olive oil now drives specialty import demand globally. Yet nothing compares to tasting a fresh varietal oil made near the olive grove just weeks prior that captures the vibrancy and nuances reflecting that estate's unique terroir in a way processing and export delays diminish.

This reinvigorated artisanal pride and all it represents - from family farm preservation to regional identity to quality ingredient integrity - suggests olive oil will remain deeply embedded in Mediterranean food culture and rural community fabric for ages to come just as it has for over 6000 years.

Olive Oil

Chapter 1

A Brief History of Olive Oil Production in the Mediterranean

Olive oil's history in the Mediterranean spans thousands of years, intricately tying into the rise and fall of civilizations that shaped this region and defined so much of Western culture. Though the olive tree's origins remain shrouded in mystery, its precious oil has left an indelible mark on cuisine, medicine, technology, religion and economy since ancient times.

This chapter traces olive oil's enduring lineage in the Mediterranean basin, the innovative production techniques that evolved over eras, and the growing globalization of this commodity that paradoxically renewed interest in artisanal, small-batch oil.

From sustaining villages to founding empires, olive oil indeed transformed societies as many societies transformed the olive oil trade through periods of scarcity and abundance. Regardless of its fluctuating availability, olive oil maintained medicinal, spiritual and social footholds nobody could displace. That enduring legacy continues today.

Origins in Antiquity

Far back into antiquity, wild olive trees likely populated Persian and Syrian regions neighboring the eastern Mediterranean coastlines near Mesopotamia and the Levant area. Archaeological evidence suggests olive tree cultivation from grafting and deliberate planting emerged during the Early Bronze Age (3500 BCE).

Remains of crushed olives discovered in Jordan and Israel point to 6,000 years ago as a probable dawn of true olive oil production. However, recent evidence at a Dalmatian Coast site hints small-scale production occurred possibly 1000 years earlier.

Most evidence confirms the Ancient Egyptians, Phoenicians and Philistines were among groups who turned nascent olive harvesting and oil-making techniques into a centralized industry between 4000 - 3000 BCE. Egyptians first adopted wild Palestinian olives using the oil in lamps, medicines and production of textiles, metals and cosmetics by at least 3000 BCE before cultivating their groves.

Tablets and texts illustrate that the Phoenicians, with their vast Mediterranean trade networks and shipping routes, introduced olive trees through Greece to Iberia/Spain as far back as 2500 BCE. They likely brought cultivation knowledge from Egypt and the Middle East.

This transformed societies they encountered, providing sustenance, wealth-building commodities and technological advancements like lamp oil to emerging settlements. Spanish olive oil would become a world dominator millennia later.

References to olive trees, with reverence to their wood and oil, abound in early religious texts of Judaism, Christianity and Islam. The Bible's Book of Genesis narrative about Noah's release of a dove from the Ark makes mention of an olive tree branch representing peace and God's blessing. Moses commands people to bring "clear oil of pressed olives" along with other offerings to the Tabernacle.

The sprawling olive tree gardens at Gethsemane, meaning "olive press", believed to date back 4000 years to Jesus' era still stand as living testaments to ancient cultivation.

By the time Classical Greece arose into cultural prominence in the first millennium BCE, olive tree agriculture was firmly established around the Aegean region. Athens became a renowned exporter and the Greeks perfected production methods still mimicked. Greek physician Hippocrates prescribed olive oil for numerous ailments. Homer's Odyssey waxes poetic about olive oil's multi-tasking utility from lamp fuel to wood treatment.

Greek sports champions were anointed in oil. Groves dedicated to Athena, the goddess of wisdom remains emblematic of enduring Greek olive oil pride—their pioneering clay amphorae with elegant painted designs transported oil by sea near and far.

Ancient Romans elevated olive appreciation into sheer reverence integrating olive oil thoroughly into society by 100 BCE after conquering Greek territories a century earlier.

Author Fabrizia Lanza notes they planted groves across the empire from Spain to North Africa to the Levant appropriating much Eastern knowledge into Roman horticultural manuals. Oil became integral to Roman cooking. They also innovated advanced cultivation, harvesting tools and milling technology while establishing large plantations called Latifundias farmed by slaves.

According to Olive Oil Times Publisher Curtis Cord, the Roman aristocratic class possessed such "obsessive connoisseurship" for fine oils that vintages were racked like wines in terracotta containers called Amphoriskos denoting estates and production year then shipped across the Empire. Some Amphoriskos found in ancient Roman shop ruins even tilted customers to optimum pouring angles.

By 300 CE, Rome's olive trade represented major economic prowess and global domination that would fade by the 6th century. Yet Roman oil production legacy and infrastructure endured for centuries after the Empire crumbled, notably in North Africa and Spain, helping spread cultivation techniques into Europe.

The Islamic golden age between 700 - 1500 CE kept focus on the eastern Mediterranean, Middle East and North Africa where science and sophisticated agriculture thrived amid the decline of western European olive oil output following Rome's fall.

Islamic nations continued cultivating olive trees through the Middle Ages developing advanced horticultural and irrigation methods adopted broadly later. Religious scripts exalting olive oil, its lore and many uses circulated widely, including promoting olive oil in Regular consumption of quality extra virgin olive battle wounds to fight infection.

Middle Age Production: Eastern Dominance to European Recovery

As Rome's formidable olive oil production collapsed between 400-700 CE due to invasions weakening its infrastructure, Arab conquerors filled the void by proliferating olive trees and oil output notably in the Levant and North Africa. Olive oil trade and production centered mostly on the oil reached its peak under the Umayyad caliphate engaging massive, sustainably farmed groves.

The Moorish conquest of Spain beginning around 700 CE reintroduced advanced olive production that the Visigoths and post-Roman rulers had increasingly abandoned. Islamic Spain eventually housed over 100,000 olive tree orchards irrigated by sophisticated channels flowing from rivers.

Muslim oil makers introduced technological novelties like hydraulically-pressed mills and heavier millstones improving paste grinding. This spurred the resurgence of Spanish oil outcompeting early Medieval Italy.

By 1300 CE, grains and olives represented Spain's most important crops thanks to Moorish agricultural leadership. Olive oil became integral to Spanish cuisine. When Christian conquerors finally expelled the Moors fully by 1492, Spain claimed over 150 million well-established olive trees producing quality oils.

In contrast, much of Western Europe, particularly the former olive belt regions of Italy and Greece, saw sharp declines in oil production for centuries after the fall of Rome due to invasions disrupting infrastructure. Rural subsistence farmers maintained meager olive tree orchards for household use but large-scale oil production dwindled.

Olive oil effectively disappeared from more northerly European diets for nearly 500 years. Those desiring olive oil depended on Arab imports trickling in at premium costs if at all.

By 1100-1300 CE, Italian monks and noble families initiated the Western European olive revival by importing materials and Arab know-how to establish monasteries and estate orchards mainly for lamp fuels and medicinal oils, but also seeking food self-sufficiency.

The influential Benedictine Order with its network of monasteries centered around Monte Cassino helped reintroduce Roman methods of intensive olive tree propagation from cuttings.

This required patience as trees need at least five years before substantially bearing fruit. Olive oil remained an exclusive luxury outside aristocracy and convents until nearly 1600.

Post Middle-Ages: Renaissance to Industrial Revolution

Full revival began in the late 14th century when Spain, Portugal, France and Italian city-states gradually reclaimed territories formerly under Moorish and Byzantine control thereby inheriting old olive tree stock. Spanish and Portuguese trading networks spread cultivation across the Americas and Asia.

By 1500, Italy pushed aggressively into commercial production to supply European demands. Sicily and coastal Tuscany led initial growth which exploded after 1600 when yields per tree increased sharply following the discovery of America and the Colombian Exchange bringing New

World crops like maize, tomatoes and peppers into the Mediterranean. These boosted regional food outputs supporting population booms that could consume more olive oil.

Olive oil supply shifted from scarcity to abundance between 1600-1850 satisfying expanding populations olive oil was used for frying new foods, in soaps, wool and fabric production and as lamp fuel enabling industries to run longer workdays.

Olive mill technology innovations increased efficiency. Hydraulic presses developed in 1700s Tuscany followed by steel lever presses in 1800s France brought continuous mechanical automation ending old, laborious beam-style presses and stone mills requiring animal or human power.

Yet olive tree agriculture remained highly decentralized with oil production occurring on small farms around hillside orchards traditionally for centuries more. Industrial consolidation and commodity grading came later. By the mid-1800s, revered oils branded by their regions such as Tuscan, Ligurian, or Provencal enjoyed fame for their flavors and perfume-like bouquets setting benchmarks.

Competitions judged by aroma and taste for extra virgin olive oils emerged in the late 1800s cementing ideals for premium quality.

Late 19th Century Shifts: Commercialization & Competition

By 1870, rapid modernization allowed large commercial groves to spread beyond traditional small farms changing landscape and supply chains. Agricultural science and technology investments occurred in universities across Spain, Italy and France seeking to improve yields, oil quality and shelf life. Grove irrigation and fertilization supplemented old dryland farming methods.

State-funded oil chemistry labs analyzed extraction methods and oil purity. Better storage tanks and bottling equipment preserved flavors. Rail transport enabled large oil cargos to move efficiently across countries replacing horse carts.

By the late 1800s, countries across Southern Europe rushed to establish modern olive tree plantations and build huge mills - particularly across Spain, France, Italy and Greece - seeking to serve booming international demands as populations and incomes rose. Table olive and olive oil imports into North America, England, Germany and Russia surged. With olive oil still used broadly in food preparation, lighting, cosmetics, lubricants and medicine, countries raced to expand cultivation beyond traditional small groves.

New steam and later electric-powered hydraulic presses and decanter-style steel centrifuges allowed continuous processing of olive paste, displacing laborious beam presses. Solvent extraction methods were introduced in some large mills to chemically force more oil from pomace though this decreased flavor. Lighter colored, blander oils flooded markets decreasing prices.

Yet tastes touted single-origin oils from small groves produced in traditional manners. Algeria's specific microclimate and conditions lent unique smoothness to its oil by 1900 though output was small. Similarly, famed Nyons olive oil from the compact Provençal town's tiny black olives persisted solely as a well-guarded regional signature taste in France despite industrialization trends.

By 1900 the entire olive landscape transformed into commercialized big business. Spain led global production reaching 175,000 metric tons by 1910 followed by Italy with 95,000 tons although the US, England and Russia relied chiefly on Italian imports through 1920.

Table olive demand grew in new Anglo-American consumer markets while olive oil for cooking and soap-making defined Mediterranean demand. With breakthroughs in tinning and later stainless steel storage, olive oil became less perishable expanding export opportunities. Pure olive oil started replacing animal fats in European kitchens.

Yet the risks of the commercial boom and Spain's deep freeze of 1956 that devastated groves revealed overreliance on monoculture cash cropping. By contrast, France's AOC system begun in the 1950s preserved small farm integrity and oil distinctiveness based on geography.

Italy, Greece and North Africa echoed similar patterns on a smaller scale maintaining localized family farm traditions while upsizing operations and incorporating modern milling allowed a competitive advantage that benefited export bans when extra virgin prices spiked after bad harvests.

The late 20th century's rise of multinational food companies and the seeding of vast tracts of imported olive varieties increased output but created new quality challenges. The pendulum swung back towards artisanal production in the 1990s among premium boutique estates. This heritage renaissance continues today retaining unique local flavors that reveal olive oil's enduring soul.

While modernization and industrialization continue influencing production scales and techniques today, what remains clear is just how profoundly important olive cultivation and olive oil extraction have been over at least six millennia in the cultures cradling the Mediterranean Sea. This sets the stage for seeing how 21st-century customs continue prizing endemic olive varieties, estate-specific growing conditions and both artisanal and large batch production methods that balance traditional integrity with today's commercial opportunities.

Olive Tree

CHAPTER 2

Varieties, Grades and Labeling

With thousands of years of olive cultivation occurring around the Mediterranean, it comes as no surprise that hundreds of named olive cultivars exist. Yet each regional variety carries unique stories, flavors and nutritional qualities beyond simply oil yield efficiency over other strains.

Far more than wine grapes, olive tree types profoundly shape oil characteristics through their biological signatures and equally importantly, growing conditions impart subtle regional distinctions called terroir reflected in their oils.

Combined with pressing techniques and timing considerations during fruit ripening stages, these variables allow single estate extra virgin olive oils their personality and complexity.

Standardized labeling categorizes baseline quality levels and production factors to aid consumers. Butlabels tell only part of the story behind an oil's depth. The rest unfolds through tasting, and understanding olive origins.

Major Olive Varieties & Flavor Profiles

There exist over 2,300 known olive cultivars though far fewer represent significant commercial production. Less than a dozen dominate globally as hardy, high-yield producers (though not always the best oil quality). Regionally another 50 varietals commonly headline boutique oils or specialty blends with the best capturing local terroir.

- **Leading Global Varieties**

Arbequina - Originally cultivated in Catalonia, Spain; Small, highly aromatic fruit with delicate pulp favored for smooth, mild oils with almond, green tomato and citrus notes. Also grown across Latin America and California. High yields but bruised easily. The world's most widespread high-density "supertree" planting olive.

Coratina - The most common olive grown across southern Italy valued for robust oil with intense grassiness, bitterness and pungency. Also lends strong herbal flavors buttery and crisp sensations coveted for finishing drizzles over dishes or bread dipping. Thrives in hot dry climates and resists olive fly damage.

Frantoio - The leading Italian table olive features heavily in oil blends for its mild, lightly herbal and nutty expressed flavors. Medium pungency and bitterness help balance other varietals while maintaining a buttery texture. Common across central Italy and Tuscany. Good frost resistance.

Leccino - Another Italian table olive also prized for velvety textured sweet oils and buttery flavor mixing well with more pungent oils that need mellowing. Tends mild displaying fresh green tomato, nutty and grassy notes. Withstands heat and lighter soils but is susceptible to fungi and olive flies making it a risky monovarietal.

Picual - The world's most planted olive hail from Spain is valued for very high oil yields and extreme hardiness tolerating late freezes and droughts. The flavor profile trends aggressively grassy, bitter and pungent while remaining fruity. The greenness amplifies other ingredient flavors making it the choice for strong finishing oils or cooking applications. Dominates Spanish and Californian production.

While the big five global varieties have valuable traits suiting modern intensive olive farming, many small estates focus exclusively on native cultivars that capture subtle local microclimates and soil conditions in their flavor. Italy claims at least 500 unique varieties boasting the greatest domestic olive germplasm and eliciting immense pride in regional uniqueness commanding designations like Protected Designation of Origin.

Lesser known Greek, Tunisian, Algerian, Moroccan, Turkish and Middle Eastern varieties remain equally endemic with backstories connecting generations through landscapes. Even thinking dominant Spanish varietals like Picual or Hojiblanca, there exist clones like Picual de Jaén uniquely expressing that province's calcium-rich soils and extreme weather shifts during ripening. Seek these special gems out!

- Other Regional Varietal Highlights

Greek Koroneiki - The highly revered regional varietal of Greece always plays a dominant role in their finest oils. Tiny Koroneiki olives grown on rocky hillsides lend medium intense bitterness paired with strong grassy notes, a peppery kick hints of citrus and nuttiness. The healthiest oils. High polyphenols.

French Picholine / Lucques - A mainstay green olive and oil variety of the AOC-regulated south France regions producing signature soft, delicate flavors with butter, nuts and light spice against gentle bitterness.

North African Chemlali - Tunisia's leading cultivar produces almost exclusively robust, fruity and grassy regional oils since Roman era planting. Composes 75% of Tunisian oil. Also grown across nearby Algeria and Libya.

Turkish Gemlik & Ayvalik - Represent over 75% of Turkish olive production. Both produce oral aromatic oils; the former balancing mild sweet nuttiness and grassy undertones; the latter offering subtle spice and apple fruitiness to its green olive tones suiting finishing, dipping and salad dressings well.

With hundreds of heritage and modern cross-breed olive varieties thriving across microclimates linked to the Mediterranean many more unique flavor experiences await discovery by adventurous, inquisitive oil enthusiasts!

Quality Classifications & Grades

Unlike wine or cheese where aging intensity defines quality hierarchies, olive oil classifications rely strictly on production and processing factors plus chemical metrics confirming freshness and proper fruit ripeness. Labels simply signal minimal quality thresholds, not necessarily overall excellence akin to rating rankings that many olive oils now display from certifying bodies and competitions.

The International Olive Council trade group defines most commercial classifications while the European Union regulates labeling and quality criteria. U.S. and other countries defer to EU standards generally.

Extra Virgin Olive Oil (EVOO) Grade - This premium quality represents the oil from the first cold pressing of olives by mechanical methods without any chemical treatment. Made under specific conditions to be absent of flaws while displaying ideal flavors and aromas of fresh olive fruit.

Acidity must equal less than 0.8% with higher polyphenol and antioxidant content when fresh. Overall EVOO offers rich sensory properties and the most health benefits compared to lesser grades. Certification programs verify production control points on accredited EV estates.

Virgin Olive Oil - Also derived from first mechanical pressing but riper fruit with acidity 0.8-2%. Minor flavor flaws are allowed. Less stringent monitoring than EVOO. Since no chemical intervention boosts yield, retains decent nutrient levels so fine for cooking and dressing though lacking EVOO's peak freshness and polish.

Ordinary Virgin/ Lampante Virgin Oil - Made like above grades but olive fruit quality or processing issues degrade acidity between 2-3.5%, considered defects. Bitterness or fusty flavors mean strictly for refining losing all nuance. Lamp oil usage gives this largest commercial-grade its name.

Refined Olive Oil - After solvents and filters remove impurities from lampante stocks, flavors become null. Processing strips all original characters though not nutrients. Mixing with cold-pressed virgin oils later restores some flavor for consumers not value full fruitiness in cooking applications.

Olive Oil / Pure Olive Oil - The ambiguous everyman grade that mixes refined olive oil with virgin grades at the

80/20 ratio by law. The blend plausibly resembles "pure" EVOO profile after adjusting chemistry. It offers decent affordability for high-heat cooking losing subtlety from heavy processing. Many consumers falsely believe it remains wholly unrefined however.

Pomace Olive Oil - Hot solvents applied to ground pits, peels and pulp leftovers after pressing coax more oil from the scruffy dregs but also extract unpleasant compounds. Further industrial refinement cleans up flaws returning muted flavor so blends with virgin oil brighten pungency. Cheapest form often used in canned products or sold in bulk.

Flavors, aromas and bitterness should not decide oil grades technically though intensities naturally concentrate along the spectrum. An exceptionally lush, complex EVOO exceeds flavor expectations for the tier whereas a tired, bland one stalls at thresholds. Judges factor sensory pleasantness into awards. Conversely, a well-balanced commercial blend like pure olive oil seems flawless and pleasant while meeting legal criteria. Shopper priorities and use applications should determine which quality grade fits culinary goals and budget even if terminology appears hazy.

Standards, Certification & Labeling

Beyond required labeling like country of origin, producer details, volume, harvest year, oil type per grades above, and best before dates, additional optional labeling aesthetics and verbiage aim reassuring consumers of quality, ethics and authenticity. Seals from organic certifiers or regional appellations also verify stewardship priorities in production.

EVOO from within defined EU geographical areas may apply for PDO (Protected Designation of Origin) or PGI (Protected Geographical Indication) seals ensuring distinct terroir and traditional practices govern cultivation and processing to accentuate local character. Much like wine appellations.

U.S. 1994 NAFTA trade deal granted European producers exclusive rights to continue using certain esteemed regional names like Tuscan, Sicily or Kalamata globally.

Supplementing denomination systems, voluntary third-party evaluation bodies like the International Olive Council and American Pantry Association Operate sensory analysis testing facilities using professional olive oil tasting certification protocols to provide inspection seals and quality ranking designations annually for producers passing chemical and flavor benchmarks.

Evaluation criteria combine objective measures like acidity and subjective judging of aromatic qualities. These seals communicate commitment to excellence beyond minimum legal requirements though producers pay membership fees.

In the specialty segment, boutique organic olive oils may carry USDA or additional "Made with Organic Ingredients" seals meaning groves use zero synthetic pesticides, fertilizers or chemicals while processors avoid solvents and heat treatments during milling. Cultivation focuses on enhancing natural soil microbiology and plant defenses using cover crops, compost, botanicals and natural predators to control pests without toxic interventions along harvest and production lines.

Certification audits ensure compliance. Small-scale growers argue their traditional, low-impact methods inherently satisfy organic priorities using time-honored wisdom without needing official seals from recent bureaucracy. Yet certification opens commercial opportunities.

Ultimately, consumers find empowerment through self-education. Look deeper than certifications to verify quality suppliers matching preferences, ethics and budgets. Request tasting notes from retailers to see if personality profiles and use applications suit needs. And product freshness remains paramount for the full enjoyment of olive oil benefits.

CHAPTER 3

The Basics: Buying, Storing and Preserving Olive Oil

Selecting quality olive oils amid dizzying options starts with understanding production types, deciphering meaningful certifications relating to individual priorities beyond those marks, and crucially, checking harvest dating and storage handling along the supply chain.

Olive oil is perishable produce at heart, not a commodity shelf-stable for years like mass-bottled seed oils. The highest quality extra virgin and virgin olive oils peak in freshness within a year or two of milling if stored optimally. Their health-protective polyphenol antioxidants and aromatic integrity fade with light and heat exposure over time.

Know that even seals guaranteeing extra virgin status only validate thresholds on a pressing date, not future shelf life. Storage, transit and retailer practices greatly impact what reaches home kitchens.

Seeking oils bottled specifically from the latest fall northern hemisphere or summer southern hemisphere harvests ensures experiencing oils at their most vibrant. However, buying shrewdly also means keeping oils correctly so their shelf life potential gets fully realized.

What to Look For Buying Quality Olive Oil

Harvest Year - Check for a specific year or harvest season noted on labels when possible or the vendor can clarify. The current year is best but the previous season is also fine within a year.

Producer Date Details - Bottling dates tell more than vague "best before" years since all olive oil degrades over time after pressing. Fresher wins.

Storage Method - Dark tinted glass or even stainless steel, preferably away from light and heat. Avoid old clear glass or plastic.

Certification Seals - Credible PDO, organic, dietary seals confirm quality priorities though never definitive. Read beyond them to match supplier practices to personal needs and ethics.

Awards & Sensory Notes - for ultra-premium estate oils, accolades from recent competition sensory judging and flavor profile descriptions suggest experiential expectations.

Regional Diversity - Don't rely on mass brands. Support smaller regional estates cultivating native olives that capture terroir and traditions with passion while pioneering sustainable techniques. These oils give back.

Overall, sourcing oils bottled directly from single harvests every 12-15 months makes experiencing fine olive oil a seasonal culinary adventure akin to enjoying the vitality of fresh produce picks.

Storage Fundamentals - Protecting Shelf Life

Olive oil denatures when exposed to oxygen, heat, or light - triple threats accelerating free radical oxidation that degrades aromatic compounds, nutrients, and fresh flavors rapidly. Follow best storage practices once home.

Choose a cool dark cupboard away from stoves, dishwashers or any heat sources. Light induces faster deterioration by facilitating photooxidation so avoid illumination. Refrigeration offers an option for prolonged quality though chilliness mutes flavors initially upon reuse until warmed slightly.

Freezing extra virgin oil is not advised however due to compromised texture and negative impacts on micronutrients that emerge upon thawing. Regardless of location preferences, keep storage consistent once open.

Opt for smaller bottle sizes aligned with use patterns rather than large metal tins exposing the oil to significant air over weeks or months after initial opening. Unless having massive consumption, buy no more than a 500ml bottle per month from Groves. If needing large quantity deals, consider dividing a tin equally into smaller, sealed opaque glass bottles to limit headspace once opened. Never transfer into clear glass decanters.

Stainless steel olive oil cruets or ceramic containers make fine short term dispensing options for kitchen counters but transfer remnants back into main storage out of light afterwards. When not cooking, cap and cover open vessel oil closely. Essentially, treat olive oil like the freshly bottled fruit juice it essentially remains regarding handling day-to-day.

What ultimately serves olive oils best mirrors what keeps us healthiest - consistency, moderation, and care.

Preserving Freshness & Preventing Rancidity

Besides abiding by the ideal storage advice above, four sensory indicators signal if olive oil is degrading from age, poor handling or contamination en route to kitchens. Knowing these helps avoid rancid, inedible olive oil.

Smell - Aromas turn rubbery, mushy or like wet paper or cardboard as oils go rancid rather than reminiscent of fresh olives. This resembles oil fingerprints of old nuts or avocados left too long. If you smell something "off" then it is.

Taste - Rancid oils lose fruity flavors first leaving just bitter, unpleasant pungency on the tongue rather than balances, silkier mouthfeels and nutty undertones. Astringency increases rapidly. Just as overripe produce loses sweetness yielding sharp acidic tastes, so too does olive oil.

Texture - Smooth viscosity that coats the mouth starts feeling thin and greasy instead, losing pleasurable thickness. Proteins and fatty acids unravel as chemical changes occur, unable to maintain pleasant lubricating weight.

Appearance - Fine sediment always exists in unfiltered olive oil from natural fruit particles and polyphenols unless tampered with in processing. This looks murky initially but usually settles. Over time, thicker debris accumulation at the bottle bottom signals degradation. Oil darkens too. If noticing cloudiness worsens or smokepoints drastically decrease, likely time to purge from kitchens so unwanted compounds don't get absorbed while cooking.

Preserving quality ultimately requires consuming premium olive oils appreciatively at ideal freshness rather than taking for granted on shelves indefinitely like palm or soybean oil. Discover how seasonal freshness comparisons open new dimensions.

The world's best olive oils change annually in subtleties like wine vintages. Therefore health-conscious epicureans should explore finer selections early when their integrity peaks, then make way for next year's limit bottlings. Much gets discovered about olive oil nuances when this renewable mindset takes hold.

CHAPTER 4

Cooking and Baking with Olive Oil

When olive oil emerged historically across European and Mediterranean cuisines, cooks quickly embraced the prized fruit juice's welcoming richness and intelligent flavor pairability for all applications from salad dressings and marinades to pan frying, baking and pasta creations.

But not all olive oils lend ideally to heating while coaxing the best from raw uses requires understanding taste profiles and balancing with other ingredients. Here we explore some techniques to inspire delicious usage.

Aroma, Strength & Heat - Secrets Revealed

With cooking, always use olive oil grades and varietals intended for heat applications. While extra virgin oils spoil delicate flavors with aggressive bitterness or pepper when heated, mild pure olive oil blends maintain integrity as carriers for other ingredients.

Robust Spanish Picual or Tuscan Coratina oils likely overpower while smooth French Lucques and Italian

Frantoios elegantly perfume dishes. Know tasting styles beforehand and discern quality from the intensity.

Certain extraction methods boost polyphenol content including oils deemed HEVOO - High Extra Virgin Olive Oil - a new class gaining recognition for extra freshness and amplified health properties when unheated.

For salads and bread dipping, these premium oils deserve to feature solo after opening. Yet as phenols increase, so does bitterness, limiting cooking applications with other foods by HEVOOs.

Consider oil colors and flavors too. Along with intensity, greener pigments signify early harvest phenolic volume and intensity favorable for cru finishing but likely aggressive for high heat sautéing or baking.

As harvest timing delays for riper fruit, yellower golden oils emerge slightly more mild and buttery but sacrifice some richness and health-protective antioxidants human cells crave.

Ultimately, olive oil versatility across sweet and savory dishes blesses cooks creatively once flavors get recognized. Taste different varietals and regional styles neatly then combine them with the ingredients planning to use. Let your palate guide ideal pairings.

Premium Flavor Pairing Tips

Experiment mixing 90% mild, buttery olive oils like early Leccino or Lucques with 10% punchier late harvest Tuscan for the best marinades and dressings.

Balance hand-torn kale salads with moderate grassy Greek Koroneiki EVOO for a luscious mouthfeel cut by lemon juice with light acidity against the slight olive bitterness.

For finishing pasta primavera, salmoriglio sauce or braises melding Mediterranean vegetables like artichokes or Fagiolini, a spicy full-bodied Sicilian brings out the sweetness in both veggies and second-pressed olive juice.

Flaky fish, seafood pasta, and chicken piccata all benefit from grassy, almond Ligurian oil drizzles over plating lending silky richness and savor to pan-frying methods without overwhelming other flavors.

Robust Portuguese and hot climate chili spiked Spanish oils jazz up gazpachos, ratatouille or eggplant caponata dishes by elongating herbal vegetable notes needing strong profile contrast from olive.

Subtly fruity Provençal, Turkish or Greek oils allow chocolate, citrus and nutty desserts room for complementary nuance without bitterness stealing the show.

These suggestions illustrate how olive oil's depth emerges best when varieties synergize with dishes instead of competing redundantly. Taste, balance, enhance.

Heating Methods - Choosing Oils Wisely

Different heating techniques create advantages for olive oil depending on chemical stability considerations. Picking oils specifically suited for high-heat tasks prevents spoilage and wasted ingredients.

Pan Frying & Sauteing – Using polyphenol-rich extra virgin olive oil exceeds smoke points at lower temperatures (320-375°F) forming toxic compounds and acrid flavors. Instead, select balanced pure olive oil (4050°F) for crisp frying with light coconut milk possible for the healthiest high-temperature vegan dishes. Alternatively, finishing off pan-cooked meats, seafood or veggies by drizzling extra virgin olive oil right before serving lends rich flavor without degradation.

Baking – Virgin olive oils monophenolics degrade readily in oven conditions too making refined olive options better for cakes, bars and breads needing 350+°F to properly set while retaining clean flavors. Substitute at a 1:1 ratio with other vegetable oils like sunflower or canola. Light olive oil works perfectly for American-style banana breads and zucchini muffins too retaining moisture against sweeteners. When making traditional European hearth breads, however, quality extra virgin olive oil mixed with brewer yeast and cold fermented adds unmatched texture and crust integrity shining at center stage flavors.

Roasting – Extra virgin diversity shines coating then oven roasting or broiling vegetables (artichokes, Brussels sprouts, cauliflower), herb seasoned bone in meats, and robust fish like tuna, salmon or sardines when lingering time under dry ambient heat. Sprinkle chopped garlic, lemon zest and navigating herbs or spices first onto proteins or veggies then coat entirely with EVOO before roasting uncovered at 425°F 15-25 minutes until caramelized as the sugars gently bring out olive nuances.

Substitution Guide – DIY Olive Oil Infusions

While olive oil won't mimic other fats taste-wise directly always in recipes, consider these modifications or infuse olive oil with intended flavor profiles planning to substitute by approximate smoke points and nutrition.

Butter – Customize olive oil blending 2 parts extra light EVOO to 1 part water whisk vigorously until emulsified then chill overnight. Use for baking or pan cooking needing butter's moisture and richness. Replace butter 1:1.

For Indian cooking needing ghee, gently warm extra virgin olive oil between 200-275°F until foaming subsides then cool. Skim off sediment. Adds nuttiness replacing ghee 1:1 though smoke points differ.

Coconut Oil - For vegan baking or frying use a mild 80% refined olive oil blended with 20% higher oleic low-scent coconut oil to better match performance and fatty acid nutrition at high heat.

Infusions – Heat 2 cups olive oil with herbs like rosemary, thyme or oregano, spices like red pepper or chopped garlic, or citrus peels gently at the lowest stove temp 10-15 minutes to infuse flavors for marinades, dressings and dipping. Cool fully then strain sediment. Refrigerate for reuse. Jazz up global recipes.

Sample Recipe Inspiration

The most gratifying way to learn olive oil's range remains simply cooking favorite regional dishes as originally intended by heritage to highlight oil interplay then modifying other recipes replacing former oils with DIY olive oil infusions. This lets full flavors shine. Try these Mediterranean preparations first.

Bruschetta - Grilled country bread rubbed with cut garlic cloves then drizzled with lush grassy Italian EVOO sprinkled with sea salt.

Gazpacho – Chilled veggie puree soup with tomato, cucumber, peppers and bread cubes dressed with bold Latin olive oil.

Fattoush Salad – Mixed Mediterranean vegetables and baked pita chips tossed with EVOO, lemon juice and zesty sumac purple spice.

Mussels Escabeche – Steamed mussels tossed with olive oil, vinegar and Latin flavors served chilled as small plates.

Aegean Sea Bass – Grilled Greek sea bass with EVOO, lemon and oregano.

Pasta Margherita – Creamy tomato basil pasta with burrata cheese and olive drizzle.

Sicilian Almond Cakes – EVOO moistened almond flour cakes with lemon zest and pine nuts.

Olive Focaccia – Flatbread punched with garlic roasted olives and olive oil bath.

CHAPTER 5

Beyond Cooking: Other Uses for Olive Oil

While olive oil deserves its celebrated status as the heart of Mediterranean cuisines, its practical versatility proved invaluable across many facets of daily life since ancient times. Whether enhancing personal care routines, tackling household cleaning or use as lubricants and fuels, olive oil's intrinsic chemical properties deliver skin soothing, antimicrobial, and moisture protection abilities other vegetable oils lack.

When produced carefully to food grade standards, the same extra virgin olive oils enhancing foods multitask effectively beyond cooking across home, health, and outdoor realms.

Health & Beauty Applications

Topically, olive oil's skin compatibility and antioxidant properties drive beauty applications today as equally as thousands of years ago.

Egyptians recognized olive oil's ability to condition skin and hair appearing in historic medicinal scripts and as part of elaborate cosmetic preparations guarding against drying winds and sun damage. Olive oil's vitamin E moisturizes while potent phytochemical antioxidants called phenols fight cellular aging, skin cancers, and UV radiation free radicals.

This innate protection explains why workers harvesting olives by hand all day display remarkably fewer signs of damage on arms and faces than expected.

Today quality extra virgin olive oil endures as a premier skin and hair care ingredient within natural commercial products or homemade recipes equally. Its fatty acid composition closely resembles our skin's sebum oils making it highly bioavailable, unlike many plant seed oils. The predominance of oleic acid (Omega 9) over 65% composition appears ideal, followed by linoleic acid (Omega 6) at under 25% for holding moisture without risk of inflammation. Palmitic and stearic saturates composing 10-20% help thicken the oil's lubricating feel. These nourish superficial skin layers without clogging pores.

Most cosmetic applications rely on cooler pressed, less acidic early harvest extra virgin olive oils boasting lower free oleic acidity (under 0.5%) and higher antioxidant components derived from unripe fruit. Later harvest oils taste fruitier for cooking but sacrifice some skin-boosting prowess. Seek bottles specifically produced for natural cosmetic use adhering to stricter processing standards and testing for purity.

Usage suggestions:

Facial cleansing oil - Mix 2 tbsp olive oil with preferred essential oil/s like lavender, tea tree or geranium. Gently massage over damp skin leaving moisture-richness, not oily residue. Rinse later with a washcloth. Weekly exfoliate by adding finely ground oats.

Ultra-hydrating hair masks - Warm equal parts olive oil with coconut milk and honey. Work through clean damp hair and allow penetrating 20+ minutes before rinsing and conditioning as usual. Shine and strength improve noticeably.

Soothing shaving oil - Swap olive oil for shaving creams. Softens skin, and lubricates razors gently allowing closeness without nicks or burn potential. Rinse cleanly without pore clogging.

Luxurious bath oil - Add a palm full of aromatic EVOO into warm bathwater and relax into moisturizing benefits from head to toe. Pat mostly dry afterward and feel lasting softness without greasiness.

Home Cleaning abilities

Olive oil's broad dissolving strength against other oils and stubborn buildup makes it an exemplary eco-friendly cleaner that pulls previous chemical traces off kitchen and bathroom surfaces while fighting microbes. People don't realize olive oil structurally resists decay conferring natural sanitizing effects against viruses, fungi and bacteria without added preservatives.

Researchers confirmed olive leaf extracts and oils bearing potent phytochemical compounds like Hydroxytyrosol tally significant germ-killing action making olive oil solutions safer but effective sanitizers. They also break down old soap, grease and oil residue extremely effectively compared to other vegetable oil cleaners.

Homemade olive oil cleaning recipes:

Gently cleansing wood furniture polish - Mix 3 parts extra virgin olive oil with 1 part lemon juice shaken into an emulsified texture. Rub over stained, tired wooden surfaces with soft cloth lifting dirt gently without chemicals or risk to surfaces.

Degreaser for kitchen messes – Combine 20 oz water with 3 oz liquid Castille vegetable soap, 2 oz pure lemon juice then 1 cup extra virgin olive oil and shake vigorously to fully blend then pour into spray bottle. Spritz over countertops, appliances and backsplashes. Let set briefly before wiping away greasy residue without effort compared to harsh chemical cleaners. Rinse dishes treated afterward.

Shining stainless steel and mirrors – Olive oil gently removes ugly hard water stains, food debris and smudges from stainless steel sinks, appliances and other reflective surfaces. Put dime-size oil directly onto a soft cloth first then rub into the mark until lifting away, followed with a clean soft towel to remove oiliness and polish back the original shine.

Other Uses Beyond Kitchen & Home

Versatility travels further as olive oil performs admirably across outdoor domains from pets and livestock to plant care and seasonal equipment protection plus kid-friendly emergency solutions!

Pet skin & fur conditioning – Extra virgin olive oil nourishes dogs and cats struggling with dry, itchy skin or poor coats. Adding oils to their foods daily or rubbing into problem flare up areas brings anti-inflammatory relief and and softness when supplied regularly.

Equestrian leather treatment – Horse bridles, saddles and tack require regular oiling just like baseball mitts to maintain shape and suppleness against cracking. Using olive oil rags gives sufficient moisture protection.

Machinery & tool rust inhibitor – Lightly wiping steel garden tools, shovels, lawn mower blades and shop equipment with coats of oil helps displace moisture reducing rust and corrosion to extend use life. Reapply before winter storage.

Eco-friendly weed torch fuel - Some sustainable gardeners fill metal weed flamers with olive oil instead of petroleum-based fuels. Though less intense and slower burning, the oil flame adequately destroys unwanted growth between garden crops without toxic runoff.

Kid and baby-friendly lubricant - Common baby olive oil gently relieves stuck zippers, loosens tight-fitting rings or bracelets and extracts tiny objects put into noses and ears without any reaction risks. Keep handy for childhood antics!

CHAPTER 6

Discovering Olive Oils from the Mediterranean

Understanding olive oil requires grasping how profoundly growing conditions - the altitude, soil, climate and endemic fruit varieties - inform flavor profiles and quality expressions of oils between regions and even individual estates. We overview influential source countries revealing commonalities and standoutSVC olive oils. Consider the long view on olive oil travel.

Spain

The perennial heavyweight champion leads global production today at over 1.7 million tons annually based on prolific native olive varieties like Picual, Hojiblanca, Arbequina and Empeltre thriving across ideal climate conditions of Spain's southern latitudes. Growth is concentrated particularly along the fertile Guadalquivir Valley nourished by coastal mountains from Huelva up past iconic Cordoba and Jaen comprising Spain's olive oil capital where bulk production continues trending toward intensive cultivation and technological innovation. Yet artisanal small-batch estate producers equally drive prestige EVOO quality catering to Spanish foodie traditions like dipping bread in olive oil with meals or flamenco style tapas grazing nightlife.

Regional Taste & Terroir Differences

Andalucian - Known for big flavor intensity; Guildive, fruity with almond highlights against a backdrop of artichoke and fresh-cut grass bitterness. High in polyphenols.

Catalonian - Softer, elegant mildly floral with sweet peach and tropical hints backed by hints of wild herbs and tomato. Smooth, clean finish.

Levantine - Assertive with bitter pungency upfront rounding towards green tomato, apple and pine nut rear tasting notes. Great for marinades and salad dressings.

With a heavy Spanish restaurant presence globally, diners often first experience higher quality Spanish oils making the varietal personalities accessible introductions to regional styles suiting multiple cuisine pairings.

Italy

Ever striving to equal Spain's production might, Italy's more fragmented terrain and lighting fast motorcycle harvest crews rushing olives to small specialty frantoi mills before fruit degradation frequently garner the highest honors for overall quality and intense region-specific flavors. Italy offers more hyper-localized styles than any competitor.

Sicily, Puglia and Calabria in the South; followed by central heartlands of Abruzzo, Molise, Basilicata, Campania and Umbria regions; tapering up through olive-dense Tuscan and Ligurian groves fanning across hillside contours vividly familiar to tourists near postcard perfect fishing villages. Italy simply overflows with proudly guarded olive oil identities even village to village.

Local cultivar loyalty reigns supreme as the optimum expression conduit of microclimate variables imprinting signature profiles bottled by the estate with familiar Italian gusto and artistry.

Coratina, Frantoio, Moraiolo and Leccino dominate imports finding niche consumer followings abroad while newcomers like Intosso and Olivastra Seggianese generate buzz domestically for their distinctive bite and sweetness attributes. Seek region first when exploring Italy's finest.

Greece

The storied ancestral olive oil motherland saturated with overlapping endearing myths and legends amid gnarled, ancient trees seemingly growing askew solely to torture harvest crews each season...Greece rightfully deserves mythic status as both the spiritual and fruitful birthplace for all olive oil on Europe's periphery.

Unique conditions stress Greek olive trees constantly - poor limestone soils, dry climate, winds, and ambitious rural cohorts eschewing tractors for sheer sweat equity hustling each epic crop by hand down slopes and into remote terrain mills. All this vivid adversity translates into low yields but intensely concentrated flavor.

Little wonder then why extra virgin oils pressed predominantly from Greece's tiny Koroneiki olives raised near the coast capture such vibrant green tomato, citrus and black pepper spice intensity catapulting their global prestige as finishing oils for chefs or discerning Greek diaspora consumers craving authenticity with each baklava bite.

Beyond small batch Koroneikis, regional blends like Lakonia from the Southern Peloponnese spike chili and nutmeg accents through softer regional varieties. Even bulk oil exporters around Kalamata must respect Koroneiki content rules guaranteeing Greece EVOO always retains a far more assertive, peppery edge than its lighter Spanish and Italian counterparts.

CONCLUSION

Preserving Heritage and Future of Olive Oil

As the stories, statistics and tasting notes accrued across this handbook hope to convey, olive oil's legacy remains inexorably linked to Mediterranean identities - past, present and future. It represents far more than monetary value as a ubiquitous agricultural commodity.

Olive oil permeates souls, societies and food pathways so profoundly that the very mention instantly conjures the salt-brined amber waves of gnarled olive trees cloaking sun-drenched vistas, the earthy umbrian potency of wet pressed oil itself awaiting transport or transfer from casks into dark green vintage bottles destined for tables where so much passion and connection unfold across generations.

Beyond sheer nostalgia, the endeavor of selecting and producing fine olive oil respects intimate connections between people and land, between traditional farm life and modern economies, between generations through continuity of craft. How olive growers foster trees mirrors how families nurture each other.

This explains why commercial production statistics and polyphenol chemistry exactness alone fail to encapsulate everything extra virgin olive oil gifting us means at a deeper level. The guiding choice resides with caring consumers whether to support sterilized mass commodity approaches or sustainable small-batch growers persevering as living repositories of accrued wisdom while fighting climate and commercial headwinds.

Olive oil prospers based on understanding, accessibility and advocacy from people who use it ultimately - as a vehicle for food, for health and for celebrating life's sensory pleasures bonding us to communities across time. That compact goes both ways in continuity.

Glossary of Olive Oil Terms

Acidity - The proportion of fatty acids present, measured as oleic acid. Acidity must not exceed 0.8% in Extra Virgin Olive Oil. Acidity indicates age and possible defects.

Amphora - An ancient Roman jug with a narrow neck used to transport and store olive oil and wine. Originated in Greece

Bitterness - One of three main positive flavor attributes along with fruity and pungency used to assess olive oils by certification boards. Present to some degree in higher quality harvests with nonlinearity and balance desired, rather than excessive bitterness overpowering other flavors. Bitterness comes from phenolic compounds.

Cultivar - A cultivated variety of plant species developed and maintained through selective breeding for desired traits. Hundreds of unique olive cultivars exist. Leading internationally utilized ones include Frantoio, Coratina, and Picual. Many other heritage varieties thrive regionally.

Cold Pressed - Historically the process of grinding whole olives into a paste for pressing without heat or chemicals to extract oil while retaining flavor and nutrition. Often used synonymously with Extra Virgin today. Most modern production employs temperature controls for precision however.

Fusty Defect - A common negative flavor defect in oils made from fermented olive fruits with anaerobic fungus and yeast buildup giving off Java-like or baby diaper characteristics deemed faulty.

Milling - The process of grinding or crushing whole olives into a paste in preparation for oil pressing using granite wheels, metal blades or rollers. May occur via circular stone mills or hammer mills. Controlled timing and temperatures prevent oxidation and paste malformation for optimal paste oils.

Musty Defect - Another common oil defect when sensory analysis detects moldy, rancid or other stale wet storage characteristics unacceptable in Extra Virgin standards.

Phenolics - The broad subclass of antioxidant phytochemical compounds found concentrated in extra virgin olive oil including flavonoids, lignans and complex polyphenols protecting against oxidation or cell damage related to heart disease, inflammation, aging, and cancer risks. Phenols explain many proven health benefits.

Smoke Point - The temperature range at which vegetable oils break down releasing bluish smoke and acrid flavors from free fatty acids degrading. Extra virgin olive oils have lower smoke points around 375°F making them unsuitable for high heat cooking without burning. More refined olive oils reach 465°F.

Vertical Integration - In commercial olive oil production, vertical integration refers to single entities controlling olive tree orchards, mills and equipment for harvesting, transport, oil extraction, bottling, packaging and distribution supply chains linking farm to shelf, thus streamlining logistics and branding continuity. Large global producers utilize vertical integration at economies of scale for efficiency, though smaller producers argue this displaces traditional participants.

Printed in Great Britain
by Amazon

40467874R00042